WOMEN ON THE US HOME FRONT

WOMEN ON THE US HOME FRONT

ESSENTIAL LIBRARY OF
**WORKD
WAR II**

Essential Library

An Imprint of Abdo Publishing
abdopublishing.com

BY KARI A. CORNELL

CONTENT CONSULTANT

RUTH MCCLELLAND-NUGENT
ASSOCIATE PROFESSOR OF HISTORY
GEORGIA REGENTS UNIVERSITY

abdopublishing.com

Published by Abdo Publishing, a division of ABDO, PO Box 398166, Minneapolis, Minnesota 55439. Copyright © 2016 by Abdo Consulting Group, Inc. International copyrights reserved in all countries. No part of this book may be reproduced in any form without written permission from the publisher. Essential Library™ is a trademark and logo of Abdo Publishing.

Printed in the United States of America, North Mankato, Minnesota

052015
092015

THIS BOOK CONTAINS
RECYCLED MATERIALS

Cover Photo: M. Marshall/US National Archives and Records Administration
Interior Photos: M. Marshall/US National Archives and Records Administration, 1; US Air Force, 3, 54; Russell Lee/Library of Congress, 6; AP Images, 10, 48, 53, 58, 60, 83, 85; Howard R. Hollem/Library of Congress, 13; Myron Davis/Getty Images, 15; John Lindsay/AP Images, 16, 98 (bottom); Hulton-Deutsch Collection/Corbis, 18; Tom Sande/AP Images, 22; Library of Congress, 25, 29 (top), 43; Bettmann/Corbis, 27, 36, 42, 51, 57, 64, 76, 80, 93, 95; Warren K. Leffler/Library of Congress, 28, 97; Alfred T. Palmer/Library of Congress, 29 (bottom), 30, 32, 41, 90, 99 (left); J. Howard Miller/US National Archives and Records Administration, 38; John Collier/Library of Congress, 47, 98 (top); John Florea/The LIFE Picture Collection/Getty Images, 66; Matson Photo Service/Library of Congress, 69; John Rooney/AP Images, 73; Abe Fox/AP Images, 75; Lt. Victor Jorgensen/US National Archives and Records Administration, 86, 99 (right)

Editor: Nick Rebman
Series Designers: Kelsey Oseid and Maggie Villaume

Library of Congress Control Number: 2015931037
Cataloging-in-Publication Data

Cornell, Kari A.
 Women on the US home front / Kari A. Cornell.
   p. cm. -- (Essential library of World War II)
Includes bibliographical references and index.
ISBN 978-1-62403-796-2
1. World War, 1939-1945--Women--Juvenile literature. 2. Women veterans--Juvenile literature. I. Title.
940.54--dc23

2015931037

CONTENTS

In the 1940s, radio broadcasts were among the most common ways people received news.

A NATION AT WAR

For most Americans, December 7, 1941, began much like any other Sunday. Mothers were in the kitchen, scrambling eggs and making toast for breakfast, shouting out to their kids, who were just stumbling out of bed. Fathers grabbed the newspaper off the front step and sat down at the kitchen table with a cup of coffee to read the latest news. War was raging in Europe, but President Franklin D. Roosevelt had refused to send American troops into battle.

It wasn't until the afternoon, when families were gathered around the table for Sunday dinner, chatting and listening to the radio, that Americans realized the significance of this day. At around 2:30 p.m. on the East Coast, the angry, excited voice of reporter John Daly interrupted the regular radio programming: "The Japanese have attacked Pearl Harbor Hawaii by air, President

Roosevelt has just announced. The attack also was made on all military and naval activities on the principle island of Ohau [Oahu]."[1]

In homes across the United States, men and women fell silent and turned up the volume of their radios. At this moment, Loa Fergot, then a young girl, distinctly remembers her mother starting to cry. Loa's brother was a college student, and she knew her mother must have been thinking of him. This terrible news could mean only one thing: surely the United States would enter the war in Europe. And that meant the government would call on more young men to serve their country in this time of need.

A NATION CAUGHT OFF GUARD

As with many other big events throughout the history of the United States, those who lived through it remember exactly where they were and what they were

THE DEVASTATION OF OAHU

Betty McIntosh, who worked as a reporter for the *Honolulu Star-Bulletin* in 1941, covered the Pearl Harbor attack. She wrote an account of what she had seen in the week following the bombings, but the story was never published because the newspaper editor thought it would be too upsetting to readers. The story was finally published in the *Washington Post* on December 6, 2012. McIntosh wrote: "For seven ghastly, confused days, we have been at war. To the women of Hawaii, it has meant a total disruption of home life, a sudden acclimation to blackout nights, terrifying rumors, fear of the unknown as planes drone overhead and lorries shriek through the streets."[2]

doing on December 7, 1941. Myrtle Fortun, a telephone operator, would never forget that afternoon. In her diary she wrote:

> *Was listening to the radio this PM. So peaceful when all of a sudden the music was broken off and an angry, excited voice said "Japan attacked Pearl Harbor without any warning." . . . Wish I was a man . . . and I sho' nuff would give 'em "L." But guess the women will be able to do their share. They always have before and we aren't so soft as not to at least try.[3]*

Thirteen-year-old Lucy Veltri was watching a movie when the film stopped abruptly and the lights came on. The theater manager made his way to the stage and announced the news about Pearl Harbor. "It frightened me so much, I don't remember what else he said," Lucy recalled. "In fact . . . I can't remember what the movie was. I ran all the way home."[4]

In many theaters, the lights went dim again and the movie resumed. But like Lucy, many people found they were no longer in the mood for a movie. They stood, gathered their coats and hats, and slowly made their way out of the theater and into the street, clearly in shock from the news.

AT THE MOVIES

In the 1940s in the United States, going to the movies was one of the most popular forms of entertainment. And from 1911 until 1967, movie theaters served another important purpose— they were a place to get the latest news updates. In the age before every American household had television, the ten-minute news clips that played before the feature movie offered viewers a glimpse of what life was like on the front lines. These clips, with names like *News of the Day* and *Eyes of the World*, were structured much like a newspaper, providing six or seven news stories in each newsreel. Big breaking news stories, such as the bombing of Pearl Harbor, filled the full ten-minute report.

President Roosevelt, wearing a black armband in memory of the victims of the Pearl Harbor attack, signs the declaration of war on Japan.

The surprise attack on Pearl Harbor caught the entire nation off guard. Although US relations with Japan had been sour for some time, no one expected Japan to attack the Hawaiian Islands. But on that fateful day in early December, Japanese planes dropped bombs on the unprepared American forces for two hours. More than 2,000 soldiers died, and more than 1,000 sustained injuries.[5]

Fortunately, the most important ships in the US Navy's fleet—the aircraft carriers—were spared, as they were away from the base during the devastating attack. This fact provided the navy and the nation with a glimmer of hope that it would be able to rebound from the attack relatively quickly.

On the next day, December 8, the United States declared war on Japan. Once again, Americans crowded around their radios to listen as Roosevelt addressed the nation. "No matter how long it may take us to overcome this premeditated invasion, the American people in their righteous might will win through to absolute victory," Roosevelt said.[6] It was official: the United States was now a nation at war.

GEARING UP TO FIGHT

Two years earlier, in 1939, the US Congress had set aside $552 million for national defense. Then, in September 1940, Congress instituted the Selective Training and Service Act, requiring all men ages 21 to 36 to register for the military draft. All drafted men were to report for duty within weeks of receiving notification of induction. With funds already reserved for the war effort and the draft in place, the United States was able to respond quickly to the attack on Pearl Harbor. War preparations were kicked into high gear.

CLASSIFICATION 3A

After the United States declared war on Japan, young American mothers held tightly to one hope: that their husbands would be overlooked for military service under a 3A classification. When the United States got involved in the war in late 1941, men with young children could be deferred from military service under the terms of this classification. In 1943, however, when the government needed more men to fill the ranks of the armed forces, fathers previously deferred under 3A were now eligible for the draft.

During World War II, nearly 39 percent of the men and women in the armed forces volunteered to serve on their own account.[7] Over the next several months, mothers, wives, sweethearts, sons, and daughters would make the early morning trek to the platform at the nearest train station to say tearful good-byes to loved ones who were joining the ranks. By the end of the war, 10 million American servicemen would head off to the war front.[8] More than 400,000 of those would never return, leaving wives and sweethearts back home to figure out how to build new lives on their own.[9]

AMERICAN WOMEN ANSWER THE CALL

The women left behind, however, did not sit by idly and wait for the war to end. By necessity, the war pushed American women who had previously not worked out their front doors and into service for the war effort, forever changing their role in society. As factories around the country retooled to produce wartime necessities during World War II, more than 400,000 women left the home to begin manufacturing weapons, ammunition, ships, planes, and other supplies needed on the front lines.[10]

For the many women who had already worked outside the home—mainly unmarried middle- and working-class women—the war opened up opportunities for heavy industrial jobs. These positions offered better pay than the jobs that were traditionally available to women at the time, such as positions at textile plants or food processing plants. African-American women, who had previously been limited to housekeeping and child care positions, were now able to find work in wartime factories or the armed forces.

A woman in Fort Worth, Texas, operates a machine that makes parts for military airplanes.

A VISUAL REMINDER

In towns and cities around the country, "honor roll" kiosks were erected near the courthouse or in town squares. These displays included a complete list of the men and women from the community who were serving overseas. When a service member died, a gold star was placed next to his or her name, a visual reminder of those lost in battle. Blue stars were also placed in the front window of each service member's family home. Richard Carlton Haney, author of *When Is Daddy Coming Home?*, was four years old in 1945, and he distinctly remembers his mother taking down the blue star from the window and replacing it with a gold one after they received word his father had died in the war.[11]

American women learned new skills and stepped up to the challenge of filling in for the men who had gone overseas. Not only did these women take on factory jobs; they also filled positions previously not available to them in journalism, business, law, medicine, science, and the military. Women also did twice the work on family farms, sewed or knit for the troops, tended gardens, joined the Red Cross, sold war bonds, or took care of neighbors' children. American women did it all—and still managed to get dinner on the table each night.

Residents of Abilene, Kansas, look at a list featuring the names of local men and women in the service.

During the war, Americans used ration coupons to purchase a wide variety of everyday items.

A NOT-SO-EVERYDAY LIFE

The attack on Pearl Harbor quickly changed the rhythm of everyday life on the US home front. The rationing of food items, for example, had a drastic effect on what women served for dinner each night. How people traveled from place to place—and whether they could travel at all—was considerably altered by the enforcement of tire and gasoline restrictions. And constant worry about loved ones overseas or possible air raids at home dampened the mood in every household.

RATIONING

On the most basic level, rationing eventually trickled down to affect nearly everyone on the home front. Within a month of the Pearl Harbor attack, the US federal government imposed rationing

restrictions on specific materials needed for the war effort. Items such as tires, bicycles, gasoline, shoes, sugar, butter, coffee, and even nylon stockings were all rationed.

In turn, every family received a rationing booklet and tokens, which spelled out exactly how much of the rationed items they were eligible to purchase each week. To ensure that everyone was following these new restrictions, the government established 8,000 ration boards throughout the country.[1]

In January 1942, with rubber in short supply, tires were the first items to be rationed. New tires were not available for purchase in the United States, and the government also urged all Americans to donate tires and other used rubber items to rubber drives that were taking

When stockings were rationed during World War II, women resorted to using coffee grounds or paint on their legs to make it look as if they were wearing stockings.

place around the country. All rubber not in use was needed to produce tires for airplanes and other wartime vehicles.

Women and children at home responded enthusiastically to these drives, scouring closets for rubber rain boots, raincoats, leaky garden hoses, and even swimming caps. Any old tires sitting around in the garage were expected to be donated. Open spaces around town became rubber drive collection sites, where a mountain of old tires and other rubber items grew until pickup day. Drives for scrap metal, paper, and clothing were also organized.

TRAVEL

Civilian automobile production was completely halted in February 1942, and gasoline rationing began in May of that year. These restrictions directly affected how Americans traveled from place to place. People were encouraged to walk short distances or take a train for longer trips. Those who took the train found

BEHIND THE WHEEL

Any unnecessary driving was strongly discouraged and considered unpatriotic. Posters and advertisements announcing these restrictions were hung all over cities and sprinkled throughout hometown newspapers and national magazines. Gas rationing was determined by need. Those who really did not need a car received an "A" mileage ration sticker, which allowed them four gallons (3.8 L) of gasoline each week. Those who could provide proof that they needed a car for the war effort—getting to work at a wartime production plant, for example—were allowed to purchase extra gasoline. Truckers received a "T" sticker, meaning they could have an unlimited amount of fuel each week.[2] In addition to rationing, speed limits were reduced to 35 miles per hour (56 kmh) in an effort to conserve gas and save on tire wear and tear.[3]

themselves jammed into very crowded cars and could expect long delays, as trains hauling troops or supplies for the armed forces were given priority. Traveling across the country often required flexibility, creativity, and at least four days of travel time. In one instance, a married woman traveling coast to coast started out in a car, switched to a train, hopped on a plane, and then finally arrived at her destination by bus. Under the circumstances, many people chose not to travel at all unless it was absolutely necessary.

THE DINNER TABLE

For American women and children, rationing began taking its most profound effect on everyday life in May 1942, when sugar and other foods began appearing on the list of rationed items. Foods such as chocolate and ice cream, which relied on sugar as a main ingredient, became largely unavailable during the war years. Foods such as bananas could not be found either, as the fuel needed to ship them across the ocean was diverted to the war effort.

By 1943, coffee, canned goods, meat, cheese, milk, butter, and other fats were also rationed and diverted to the war effort. Coffee went directly to the troops overseas, while the fats from meat and dairy products were used for making soap and ammunition. The tin used in cans was needed for wartime manufacturing.

Always resourceful, American women managed to put food on the table despite these wartime shortages and restrictions. Although canned items such as peas, for example, could be found on grocery store shelves, they were very expensive. To supplement fruits and vegetables, many families planted and tended gardens, either in their yards or in nearby empty lots. Community garden plots sprang up across the nation, with the sole purpose of growing food for the war effort. They were called Victory gardens because by tending them, those on the home front were doing their part to help the United States win the war.

At times in 1943, meat was so scarce that long lines would form outside grocery stores as people waited for their rations. In small towns, where local grocers usually knew many of the customers by name, it was common for grocers to set aside cuts of meat and other necessities for families who had loved ones in the service. This was the grocer's way of showing his appreciation for families with sons, fathers, mothers, or daughters abroad. Families also learned to supplement meat rations by raising rabbits, chickens, pigeons, and sometimes even dogs for food. Fishing and hunting put food on the table as well.

Jean Lechnir remembers having a passel of pigeons. When meat was scarce, her family would butcher a pigeon and roast it for dinner. They also tended a Victory garden and "canned everything we could get our hands on," Lechnir said. Her family ate more hamburger than usual because it was more commonly available than cuts of meat such as steaks and roasts. The family also ate "a whole lot of oatmeal," as cereal was cheap.[4]

GETTING AROUND RATIONING

As is usually the case in times of hardship, there were those who found their way around ration restrictions. People stashed canned vegetables purchased on the black market in attics and basements. Others hoarded extra gasoline in underground storage tanks. And it was at about this time that restaurants stopped leaving full sugar bowls and sticks of butter on tables because people would steal them. Individual sugar packets, jam packets, and prepackaged pads of butter took the place of the larger portions of these rationed items. Theft and hoarding of rationed items was illegal and considered unpatriotic. This theme surfaced often in posters and movies from the war years.

New York City residents wait in line to buy coffee. Each customer was allowed to buy only one pound (0.5 kg).

Wartime editions of popular cookbooks provided recipes and tips for cooking with what was available. The books showed readers how to do without items once thought of as necessities. *The Victory Binding of the American Woman's Cookbook, Wartime Edition* advised women to fill up on poultry, make more soups, and use perishable meats such as livers, kidneys, and other organs that could not be shipped overseas without spoiling. In the introduction, the book's editor offered these words of encouragement: "On the bright side is the eagerness of the modern woman to pit her intelligence against a knotty problem. She will need to learn not only to prepare all the food needed in her household, but to raise her own garden and poultry and save every last bit, as has not been done in several generations."[5]

BLACKOUTS

In the aftermath of the Pearl Harbor attack, an undercurrent of fear spread across the nation. Worry about war took the strongest hold on the West Coast, where people felt especially vulnerable to enemy attack. The precautionary actions taken in West Coast communities added to the sense of danger. For example, on December 8, 1941, families and businesses in every town and city in western Oregon were ordered to douse their lights and follow blackout restrictions. The rationale was that enemy planes would have a more difficult time bombing a city if all the city's lights were out.

Even people in small towns in the Midwest lived in constant fear of bombings. In the December 15, 1941, issue of the *York News Times*, the newspaper for the town of York, Nebraska, an article was titled "What to Do in an Air Raid."

It instructed readers to do three things: "1. Keep Cool, 2. Stay Home, 3. Put Out Lights."[6]

The first blackout drills were held even before the United States entered the war. The US Office of Civilian Defense, which formed in May 1941, ordered blackout drills. Posters hung all over Portland, Oregon, weeks before a scheduled drill on October 31. This meant all lights out, with no exceptions. Families prepared by hanging special curtains that prevented any inside light from showing through to the street. Restaurant signs and lights were extinguished. No headlights from cars, no streetlights—not even the glow from a cigarette could be visible. Multnomah County, which includes the city of Portland and surrounding communities, reported that 8,000 "lady air raid wardens" helped with the drill.[7]

After war was declared, blackout drills took place regularly all over the United States. In Saint Louis, Missouri, at precisely 10 p.m. on December 14, 1942, emergency sirens and factory whistles blared, announcing a blackout drill that

LOOSE LIPS SINK SHIPS

Worried that enemy spies might be living within the United States and listening to every conversation, the Office of War Information warned all Americans on the home front to keep their lips sealed. For the women and children left behind, this meant they could not discuss news of ships sailing or aircraft departing, even within the context of talking about their loved ones who were heading overseas. For the men in uniform, this meant they were not allowed to mention troop movements, battle outcomes, or even where they were stationed in letters home or in everyday conversation. On lampposts and community bulletin boards, and in back alleys of cities and small towns all across America, graphic posters reminded citizens of the dangers of talking about the war. "Loose Lips Sink Ships" was one of many phrases used on such posters.

A woman installs boards in her windows to block the light. This procedure had the added benefit of improving insulation, which enabled the homeowners to save on heating costs.

was taking place across seven states in the Midwest. Volunteer air-raid wardens strictly enforced the rules. For several weeks before the drill, 7,500 Civilian Defense program volunteers walked through neighborhoods, distributing fliers to families with detailed instructions for how to prepare for the drill.[8]

AIR-RAID DRILLS

An air strike in any part of the United States was unlikely. Nevertheless, Americans could not help but think about the newsreel clips that showed the devastating bombing of London, England. All Americans on the home front became well versed in identifying enemy aircraft from the ground. Families were encouraged to practice air-raid drills at home, which meant hiding under kitchen or dining room tables. Families were also encouraged to have a plan in place for where they could take shelter in case of an air raid. In many households, women kept a supply kit ready. These kits typically consisted of canned food, water, blankets, candles, and matches.

Schools also staged air-raid drills regularly, and many mothers volunteered to help as School Defense Aids (SDAs). During the drills, SDAs helped teachers keep order as students crouched under their desks or lined up and followed the teacher into the hallway to sit down against the wall. Women reassured their children that they were safe and that bombs would not fall on their hometown. But they also took comfort in knowing they had done everything they could to prepare for possible attacks.

Barbara Williams Roberts, a schoolgirl living in Clinton, New York, during the war, remembers the first air-raid drill at her school on February 26, 1942: "It was scary. I was still in grade school, and I remember hearing an airplane and looking up to see what it was. I think I expected the Japanese to bomb Clinton."[9] In these frightening moments, American mothers set aside their own worries to ease their children's fears and offer comfort.

Students in Seattle, Washington, take part in an air-raid drill in late December 1941.

RATIONED ITEMS
GOING WITHOUT DURING THE WAR

RATIONED ITEM	RATIONING DURATION
Tires	January 1942 to December 1945
Bicycles	July 1942 to September 1945
Gasoline	May 1942 to August 1945
Fuel oil and kerosene	October 1942 to August 1945
Solid fuels	September 1943 to August 1945
Stoves	December 1942 to August 1945

RATIONED ITEM	RATIONING DURATION
Rubber footwear	October 1942 to September 1945
Shoes	February 1943 to October 1945

RATIONED ITEM	RATIONING DURATION
Sugar	May 1942 to 1947
Coffee	November 1942 to July 1943
Processed foods	March 1943 to August 1945
Meats, canned fish	March 1943 to November 1945
Cheese, canned milk, fats	March 1943 to November 1945[10]

Women install parts on a B-17 bomber at a plant in Long Beach, California.

WOMEN GO TO WORK

Although most single women and some married women worked outside the home prior to World War II, the conflict drew more women into the workforce than ever before. From 1940 to 1945, the number of American women in the labor force increased by more than 50 percent.[1] The number of female workers during the war peaked at 19 million in July 1944.[2]

EAGER TO PUNCH IN

Women of all ages joined the workforce, and they did so for many reasons. Some worked out of a sense of patriotic duty and a desire to do their part to help win the war. From late 1942 until 1944, the Office of War Information posted advertisements in newspapers and magazines and plastered lampposts and walls with posters that appealed to this sense of patriotic duty. The posters featured slogans that tugged on the heartstrings, including "The more

The more WOMEN at work the sooner we WIN!

WOMEN ARE NEEDED ALSO AS:

FARM WORKERS	WAITRESSES	TIMEKEEPERS	LAUNDRESSES
TYPISTS	BUS DRIVERS	ELEVATOR OPERATORS	TEACHERS
SALESPEOPLE	TAXI DRIVERS	MESSENGERS	CONDUCTORS

—and in hundreds of other war jobs!

SEE YOUR LOCAL U.S. EMPLOYMENT SERVICE

women at work, the sooner we win!" One said, "Women: There's work to be done and a war to be won . . . NOW!" Another said, "Longing won't bring him back sooner . . . get a war job!"[3] Early in the war, these posters targeted mainly single women, specifically for wartime production jobs. However, as most single women had already gone to work by 1943, the ads shifted to appeal to homemakers and included civilian manufacturing and service jobs as well.

Many married women answered the call to employment, while single women were eager to embrace the new, better-paying job opportunities available to them. Half of all women with husbands in the military worked during the war years to supplement the small stipend they received from the government. Families of servicemen received a

Propaganda posters such as this one encouraged American women to take jobs that helped the war effort.

minimum of $50 per month, part of which was deducted from the serviceman's pay.[4]

For the first time in more than a decade, women had the opportunity to contribute to the family income. Americans had just climbed out of the Great Depression, a time when society frowned on women working outside the home because they were thought to be taking jobs away from unemployed men. In the 1940s, women were eager to roll up their sleeves and earn money for the household. And for the first time in history, employers were willing to hire women for positions that before the war had typically been reserved for men. Now, with men away, women responded to the call to fill those desirable jobs, which usually offered higher pay and a chance to try something new.

ON THE MOVE

Wartime jobs drew people from far and wide. An estimated 30 million Americans moved away from home in the 1940s, many to take new jobs or join the military. Many of these jobs were on the coasts, where shipbuilding and aircraft industries were located. But cities such as Detroit, Michigan, where existing industries retooled for the war effort, saw growth as well. Between 1941 and 1943, as many as 350,000 workers moved from the south and other parts of the country to work in Detroit.[5]

ON THE FACTORY FLOOR

The iconic image of Rosie the Riveter often comes to mind when people think of women working during World War II. Wearing a red bandana and blue coveralls, Rosie appeared in countless posters, magazines, and newspapers. This advertising campaign was part of an effort to entice women to work in munitions factories, shipyards, and aircraft assembly lines during the war. And it worked. Women answered the call. After relatively short, intensive training

EXECUTIVE ORDER 8802

World War II opened doors for thousands of African Americans in the workplace as well. A. Philip Randolph was a black train porter who had plans to lead 100,000 African Americans in a march on Washington, DC, to protest job discrimination.[7] This led President Roosevelt to sign Executive Order 8802 in June 1941. The order prohibited the defense industry from discriminating against applicants or employees on the basis of race, and it translated into higher paying jobs for all African-American workers. While this may have given blacks a foot in the door, discrimination still played out on a day-to-day basis on the job.

sessions lasting eight weeks or less, women were considered ready to take their place alongside men on the factory floor. Women worked hard to prove themselves and earn the respect of their supervisors and coworkers.

The line of work that saw the greatest increase in female workers during the war was, by far, the American aircraft industry. In the years before the war, women made up a mere 1 percent of workers in this industry. By 1943, that number had skyrocketed to 65 percent.[6] More than 310,000 women were employed in the industry that year. Women in the aircraft industry commonly worked in pairs. One was a riveter and the other was a bucker. The riveter used a rivet gun to shoot rivets into the sheets of steel, fastening them together. The bucker worked on the other side of the metal sheet, using a bucking bar to smooth the rivets against the metal. This was not difficult work, but it did take some upper body strength—and the women in these jobs certainly worked hard, for as many hours as needed to keep up with the workload. The whirring of the rivet guns made for a constant racket all day long, and nobody wore ear protection. Dust from the metal got into people's skin and eyes as well.

NEW OPPORTUNITIES FOR WHITE-COLLAR WORK

The shortage of male workers during World War II opened up several new opportunities for women that extended far beyond the factory floor. Women did everything from pumping gas to managing businesses. They also worked as lawyers and journalists and held civil service positions.

When male lawyers left for the front lines, women with law degrees stepped up, seizing the opportunity to practice law for the first time. Many had worked as law office secretaries before the war. And when the men who were in law school were called up for the draft, many women filled those open seats and earned their law degrees. In fact, the number of women enrolled in law schools increased considerably during the early 1940s, jumping from a mere 4 percent of students in 1940 to nearly 22 percent by 1943.[8]

Before World War II, female journalists had experienced similar limitations in their own careers. Women were typically assigned only to women's interest stories. But with the men away, female reporters covered the war effort and other more weighty topics, such as the effect of war on people at home. More than 125 female journalists received accreditation to cover news from the front lines.[9] Journalist Dorothea Lange received a government assignment on the West Coast, where she photographed the relocation of Japanese Americans into internment camps.

Other women secured work in science-based fields such as oceanography, nuclear science, and computer development. While some women who found

Eleanor Ohsol, an assistant picture editor, determined which photographs were worthy of being included in the newspaper.

work in these areas had studied the sciences, there were many jobs for which a science background was not necessarily required. Examples include jobs with the Manhattan Project or the MIT Radiation Lab, top-secret laboratories where atomic bombs and other war-related projects were in the works. Employers wanted reliable, hardworking people who could learn quickly and keep quiet about their jobs. Virginia Gerdes, who responded to an ad in the newspaper straight out of high school, worked at the MIT Radiation Lab. Gerdes took an exam to demonstrate her grasp of math and science and was placed in a position as a technician. All training was provided on the job. Gerdes and many young women like her were thrilled to find employment working 48 hours a week, making decent pay, and aiding the war effort.

WORKERS' RIGHTS

In these fast-paced times, workers' rights were often tossed out the window in the name of getting things done. Unions did exist, and women joined them when necessary, but the unions commonly provided more support for male workers than females. For example, when men returned from the war and wanted their jobs back, women were expected to simply pack up and leave. Women countered this lack of support by standing up for each other. Groups of women often went together to apply for jobs. Sometimes female workers banded together to fight against injustices as well.

INTERNMENT CAMPS

Not all American women had the opportunity to help their country during the war. For many people of Japanese descent, the war years were a dark period spent in internment camps. Many West Coast communities had been worried that Japanese Americans were not loyal to the United States, and this led President Roosevelt to sign Executive Order 9066 in February 1942. As a result, more than 120,000 people of Japanese descent were forced to leave their homes and move to internment camps.[10] Armed guards patrolled the camps, and the people inside were not allowed to leave until the war was over.

Evelyn Gotzion, who worked for a battery company, remembers a time when the company cut the pay of a group of workers for no apparent reason. She and

ROSIE THE RIVETER

The American public's first glimpse of Rosie the Riveter came in 1942, when she appeared on a poster for Westinghouse Power Company. Wearing blue coveralls with her hair tucked into a red bandana, Rosie flexes her muscles beneath the slogan "We Can Do It!" This vision of strength and perseverance convinced American women that they really could do something to help win the war. Although Rosie the Riveter was not a real person, she was based on several real-life munitions workers, including Rose Will Monroe and Rose Bonavita. On May 29, 1943, Rosie the Riveter appeared on the cover of the *Saturday Evening Post*. In this version of Rosie, painted by Norman Rockwell, she rested a rivet gun on her lap while holding a ham sandwich. The Rosie campaign remains one of the most successful means of recruitment in US history.

her coworkers organized and fought back. Gotzion volunteered to represent the group at union meetings, and they were eventually able to claim back pay.

NOT ALWAYS WELCOME

Even though women were desperately needed in the workforce during the war, they did not always feel welcome or appreciated. In many instances, women were paid less than men for the same work. Rose Kaminski, who operated a crane during the war, reports she was paid eighty cents less per hour than men who did the same job.[11]

While there were plenty of men who were supportive and offered to help women on the job site, there were also those who assumed women were not capable of the work. Some women reported instances of men discriminating against them, harassing them, and talking down to them in the workplace. It was not uncommon for a woman walking to work to endure catcalls, whistling, or demeaning remarks from men along the way. Women ignored this behavior, reported it to a supervisor, or simply moved on to a different job. In the 1940s, they had no other choices.

A SENSE OF CAMARADERIE

Many American women who found themselves working outside the home for the first time found a sense of camaraderie with the other women at work. As a group, working women had much in common. Many had husbands or sweethearts overseas, so they shared details about the letters they received or confided their worries when letters from loved ones did not come. During these trying times, young women tended to form friendships that were stronger than ever. Female coworkers who met on the assembly line or around the water cooler at the office soon began spending time together in the evenings or on days off.

Emily Koplin, who was young and single with an office job, remembers spending lots of time with a tight-knit group of girlfriends from work. Office jobs were not nearly as tiring as factory work, so the girls always went somewhere at the end of their shift, usually out to eat or to play Ping-Pong at someone's house. On the weekends, they went to movies or to United Service Organizations (USO) dances. At these dances, American women such as Koplin and her friends were encouraged to socialize and entertain US servicemen while they were in town.

TIME OFF

Time off was a precious commodity for the working woman of the 1940s. The standard eight- to ten-hour workday left little time or energy for other activities. Women often rushed to the grocery store with ration coupons during their lunch break or after their shift. Then they hurried home to get dinner on the table. Exhausted, many fell into bed around nine or ten o'clock, and then awoke early to catch the carpool back to work. The typical workweek was 48 hours, with one day off. On her first day off in eight days, Augusta H. Clawson, a welder in a West Coast shipyard, looked forward to going grocery shopping, getting a haircut, doing some mending and laundry, and writing a letter to her family. "I hate to waste precious hours of a day off on a movie," she wrote in her diary.[12]

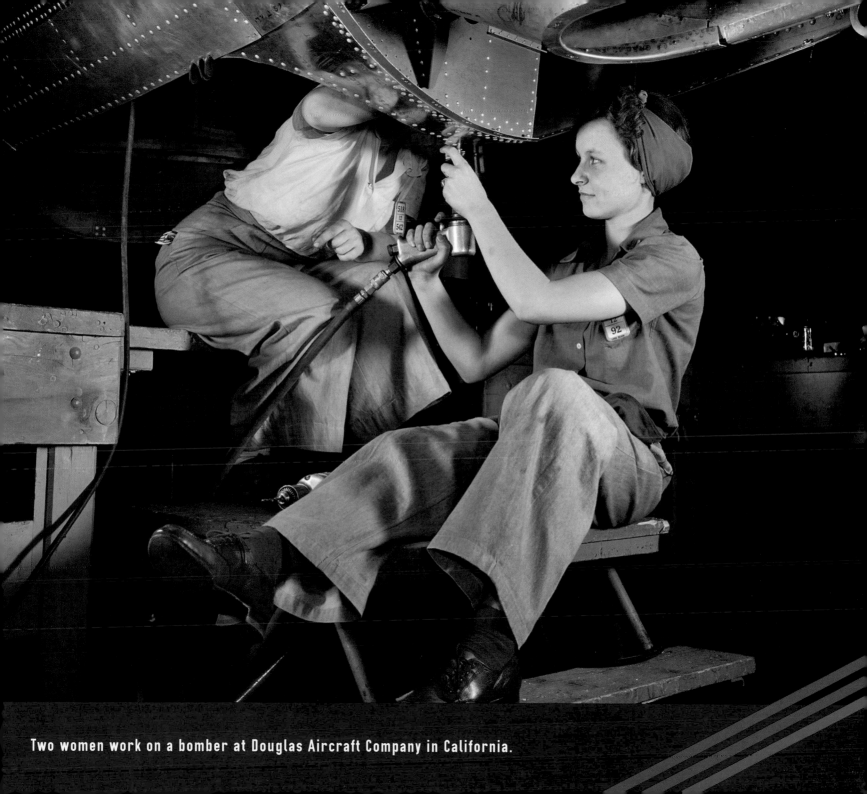

Two women work on a bomber at Douglas Aircraft Company in California.

Members of the American Women's Voluntary Service go to work in a Victory garden.

CHAPTER 4

VOLUNTEERING FOR THE WAR EFFORT

During the early 1940s, there was a strong push for women on the home front to "do their part" for the war effort. But this did not necessarily mean women had to pull on work boots and coveralls and apply for a job at the nearest munitions factory. There were countless opportunities to help right in the community, sometimes without even having to set foot outside the front door. Women planted fruits and vegetables; knit socks, caps, and gloves for servicemen overseas; mailed care packages and letters; and sold war bonds. With each of these seemingly small gestures, women made a big difference on the front lines and at home.

DIG FOR VICTORY

Because of gas and tire rationing, hauling produce from farms to grocery stores became challenging and expensive. So the government undertook a campaign to encourage all Americans to supplement rationed produce with homegrown fruits and vegetables. As it did for the drive to convince women to work for war industries, the government produced colorful posters promoting Victory gardening and home canning. Many of these posters featured young American women with slogans such as "Of course I can! I'm as patriotic as can be—And ration points won't worry me!" and "The Seeds of Victory Insure the Fruits of Peace. Victory Gardens Help the Hungry."[1]

Nearly 20 million Americans picked up shovels to turn over soil in backyards, community garden plots, empty city lots, school yards, and even on rooftops.[2] Gardens sprang up in front of City Hall in San Francisco, California; at the zoo in Portland, Oregon; at Arlington Racetrack in Chicago, Illinois; and on a busy corner in downtown New Orleans, Louisiana. The efforts of these gardeners—which included women, men, soldiers, nuns, First Lady Eleanor Roosevelt, and some movie stars—paid off. According to the US Department of Agriculture, 9 to 10 million short tons (8.2 to 9.1 million metric tons) of fruits and vegetables were harvested from Victory gardens during the war years—the same amount of veggies grown on commercial farms during that period.[3]

University extension offices, programs operated by state universities that provide practical education on a number of topics, offered training to new gardeners nationwide. *Life* magazine published articles filled with gardening tips, plans, and practices to avoid. According to *Life* editors, the ideal garden measured 20 by 40 feet (6 by 12 meters). When thoughtfully planted and well tended for seven or eight hours per week, such a garden would produce "most of a family's green vegetables for four or five months," all for an initial investment of $1.30 in seeds and $1.50 in fertilizer.[4]

American women also turned to canning to preserve foods after picking. Sales of pressure cookers used in canning rose from 66,000 in 1942 to 315,000 in 1943.[5] When it came time to can, everything had to be done in a hurry or the food would spoil. For American women, this meant many frantic days of hard work in steamy kitchens. Mary Scott took a moment to jot these thoughts in her diary on May 23, 1944, after a long day of canning: "Rain! The gardens need it bad. Canned up seven quarts carrots, and I set the alarm for 1:20 A.M. and went to bed."[6]

KNIT YOUR BIT

Eleanor Roosevelt was often pictured in newspapers and magazines looking up from her knitting needles with a smile. She was doing her part for the war effort by knitting for the troops and setting a good example in the process.

When the cover of the November 24, 1941, issue of *Life* magazine featured a

GARDENING DON'TS

The following list of simple rules was published in the March 30, 1942, issue of *Life* magazine, complete with entertaining illustrations by Helen Hokinson.

- Don't start more than you can finish.
- Don't waste good seed on bad soil.
- Don't work the ground too soon.
- Don't plant rows up and down a hill.
- Don't use too much seed.
- Don't plant too much of one thing.
- Don't let tall plants shadow low ones.
- Don't wield too heavy a hoe.
- Don't let the weed crop win.
- Don't spare the water.
- Don't let the bugs beat you to it.
- Don't let anything go to waste.[7]

ELEANOR ROOSEVELT

1884–1962

Anna Eleanor Roosevelt was born in New York City on October 11, 1884. In 1905, Eleanor married her fifth cousin, Franklin D. Roosevelt. The Roosevelts had six children, but Eleanor still found time to work for the Red Cross during World War I.

During World War II, Eleanor became a tireless champion for the poor, the disadvantaged, and women. She encouraged the managers of factories producing war goods to provide working women with day-care options and to make food available onsite. She also believed women were perfectly capable of serving in the armed forces and supported Jackie Cochran's efforts to begin the Women Airforce Service Pilots (WASP) program. In addition, Eleanor was instrumental in starting the Women's Land Army, a government program that paid women to grow food for the war effort. After her husband's death on April 12, 1945, Eleanor continued to work for the causes she believed in. In 1960, she wrote, "You gain strength, courage, and confidence by every experience in which you really stop to look fear in the face. . . . *You must do the thing you think you cannot do.*"[8] She died in New York in 1962.

picture of a young woman named Peggy Tippett knitting, thousands of women—and also men and children—picked up needles and learned to knit their first stitch, all in the name of the war effort. That issue of *Life* included basic instructions on how to knit, complete with a sweater vest pattern for soldiers. The military needed 1 million sweaters in time for the Christmas holiday.[9] At that time, the sweaters were for British and European soldiers. Little did the knitters know US soldiers would need their own sweaters and socks within a few months.

Countless knitting patterns became widely available during the war years, including patterns for socks, scarves, sweaters, fingerless mittens, vests, helmet covers, toe and stump covers to pull over casts, and many other items. Most of these patterns were published and distributed by the American Red

Women were not the only ones who knit for the troops. Many children did their part as well.

Eleanor Roosevelt, seen here knitting, often held press conferences in which she discussed women's issues, human rights, and improving the lives of children.

Cross, but private yarn companies printed their fair share as well. The Red Cross organized the knitting for the war effort, handing out free patterns with yarn. Patterns were to be knit using khaki or navy yarn, and knitters had to follow patterns precisely or the items would be rejected. The Red Cross also urged knitters to finish projects as quickly as they could.

Women knit through all idle moments to meet these needs and ensure the soldiers kept warm. They knit on the bus, through their lunch hours, and in the evening while listening to the news on the radio. Knitting bees were held around the country, where women knit together and could get help with patterns as needed. Women also gathered to knit and roll cotton bandages, lengths of tightly knit fabric used for bandaging soldiers' wounds on the battlefield. Knitting provided an easy way for women to do something significant for the war effort, on their own timeline, no matter where they were.

DEAR SOLDIER

One key responsibility of women on the home front during the war was that of cheerleader and optimist. Wives, sweethearts, and mothers were expected to put on a smile and lift spirits—not only at home but also through letters and care packages. Words of encouragement, a favorite variety of candy, or a hand-knit pair of wool mittens could make all the difference to a homesick soldier during the dreary days of war.

Women's organizations and social groups reached out to help soldiers both at home and overseas. Alice Amaro, who worked as an ammunition handler, was a proud member of the San Sausi Club, a group of women dedicated to sending care packages to US soldiers abroad. Another such group was known as WIVES, which stood for Women Insure Victory, Equality, Security. Formed by five women from New York who met at Camp Stewart, Georgia, just after their husbands shipped out for Europe, the organization grew to include chapters from all over the country. Each week, WIVES members visited veterans hospitals to socialize, play games with the patients, and deliver homemade cakes and donated clothing.

Members also got together to make care packages for their husbands. On a more personal note, the women comforted each other and provided support to members who lost their husbands in action. WIVES member Sylvia Cohen Corwin recalled that seven women from their New York chapter had husbands who were killed or missing in action.

Letter writing was strongly encouraged, as soldiers reported how much hearing from someone back home boosted morale. The US government urged Americans to write to their sons, brothers, fathers, and husbands on the front frequently about anything at all, including day-to-day activities, family news, and what was going on in their hometown. Hearing this news on a regular basis provided servicemen with a connection to home that helped carry them through hard times. And letters did not have to come from family or even friends. Some small-town newspapers posted photos of servicemen on a particular day of the week and invited readers to write letters to the men. Many pen pals who began

V-MAIL

Early in the war, cargo space on planes was used for provisions directly related to the war effort. That meant letters and packages from home were shoved into cargo holds on ships, which took weeks to cross the ocean. Then, in June 1942, the government introduced V-mail, a single sheet of lightweight airmail paper that folded into its own envelope. All letters had to go through government censors, and the V-mail letters' uniform size streamlined this step. And many more V-mail letters—150,000, in fact—could fit into one mail sack.[10] In contrast, 37 sacks were needed to transport the same number of odd-sized letters and packages.[11] This meant more mail could be delivered to the intended recipients in a shorter amount of time.

A woman writes a V-mail letter to her husband and includes a photograph of the couple's baby.

writing during the war became lifelong friends or, as in the case of Marge and Charles Vlasic, husband and wife.

SELL WAR BONDS!

Many women volunteered to sell war bonds, which were essentially loans to the government. For example, a typical war bond could be purchased for $18.75. Ten years later, the person who purchased the bond would receive $25 from the US government.[12] Between February 1942 and December 1945, 85 million Americans purchased bonds totaling $185 billion.[13]

These bonds generated money for the government to pay for the war, including building planes and ships and buying medicine and food. Members of the WIVES often sold war bonds to audiences at local movie theaters before the feature film began.

THE WAR BOND BANDWAGON

The government enlisted the help of celebrities to sell war bonds. Movie and recording stars including Frank Sinatra, Bob Hope, Marlene Dietrich, and Bette Davis performed live or on the radio in towns and cities around the country, promoting the purchase of war bonds in the name of patriotism.

War stamps were also available for twenty-five cents each and could be collected into a booklet and turned in for war bonds. The stamps were very popular with children.

BUY A BOND TODAY

Movie star Jane Withers is surrounded by soldiers as she encourages people to buy war bonds.

A flight team from the Women's Airforce Service Pilots walks from their plane, a B-17 called *Pistol Packin' Mama*.

WOMEN IN THE SERVICE

American women had served as army nurses since 1901 and as navy nurses since 1908. In World War I, they served in limited enlisted positions in the navy, marines, and coast guard. But World War II was the first time they served in all branches of the service in non-nursing capacities and the first time they served as officers in all branches of the US military.

Nearly 350,000 women volunteered for some branch of military service.[1] Women signed up despite frequent disapproval from family members—not to mention the common perception that women were too delicate for military service. The American public, especially men, held on to the belief that it was immoral for women to join the military and that military service threatened a woman's femininity. But inviting women into the military to serve

NURSE AWARDED PURPLE HEART

In the aftermath of the attack on Pearl Harbor, First Lieutenant Annie G. Fox became the first nurse to be awarded the Purple Heart, an honor usually reserved for soldiers injured or killed in action. On December 7, 1941, Fox was the chief nurse on duty at Hickam Field when the first round of injured soldiers were brought in. Working to treat the constant stream of wounded with a shortage of medical supplies, Fox remained calm in the face of panic. For her outstanding leadership and courage, Fox was recognized with this prestigious award.

in clerical positions and other noncombat jobs freed up more men to fight on the front lines. Women, however, did far more than file papers and type reports. They also drove trucks, worked as mechanics, operated radios, and repaired aircraft. Women were test pilots, flying both repaired aircraft and new jets. They also served as gunnery instructors, parachute packers, cryptographers, interrogators, and intelligence officers. And many women responded to the desperate need for nurses, both at home and overseas.

By the end of the war, women had served in all branches of service and in every place in the world where the US military was deployed. Women earned Purple Hearts and were held as prisoners of war. More than 500 American women lost their lives in World War II.[2]

WOMEN'S ARMY AUXILIARY CORPS

Immediately after the attack on Pearl Harbor, female volunteers stepped up to staff aircraft-spotting stations. These stations were located around the country but were especially common on the coasts. Working in shifts around the clock, women performed the very important job of keeping an eye on the skies for approaching enemy aircraft.

Female volunteers stand at attention at Fort Devens in Massachusetts.

In early 1941, due in large part to the tireless efforts of Congresswoman Edith Nourse Rogers, the idea of developing the first women's division of the US armed forces began to take shape. In May 1942, the US Congress established the Women's Army Auxiliary Corps (WAAC), under the direction of Oveta Culp Hobby. This monumental decision stirred protest among newspaper columnists, clergy, and many members of Congress. Despite public outcry, the armed forces began accepting women into their ranks later in 1942, simply based on the need for "manpower."

OVETA CULP HOBBY

1905–1995

Born on January 19, 1905, Oveta Culp Hobby worked as a reporter for the *Houston Post Dispatch* during the 1930s and became known nationwide as an outspoken advocate on women's issues. In June 1941, Hobby received a call from General David Searles asking if she would help organize and lead the US Women's Army Auxiliary Corps. Hobby accepted the challenge and was appointed the director of WAAC. In only three years, Hobby built the organization from the ground up, resolving countless difficulties along the way. Eventually she led 100,000 women who served in many different types of jobs all over the world. Yet she did not rise above the rank of colonel.[3]

At the end of the war, Hobby resigned from the military and went back to Texas to return to journalism. She was awarded the Distinguished Service Medal in 1945. In 1953, under the Eisenhower administration, Colonel Hobby became the second woman to hold a US cabinet position.

Adah Mae Briscoe was one of many American women who responded to the call for new recruits. Briscoe said that when she told her parents she was volunteering for WAAC, her father "had a fit," but he did allow her to go.[4] She attended boot camp at Camp Oglethorpe in Georgia and later went to Nacogdoches, Texas, to study army administration. She served in Virginia, where, from an office in the basement of the Pentagon, she was responsible for copying top-secret documents.

Women endured training regimens similar to men's, but without the weapons and war tactics classes. In July 1942, 440 officer candidates and 330 enlisted women reported for training camp in Des Moines, Iowa.[5] Forty of the officer candidates were African-American women.[6] Later that same year, the first WAACs traveled to overseas assignments, mostly in Europe, but also in the Pacific and the Far East.

In 1943, WAAC officially became part of the US Army, changing its name to the

DAILY SCHEDULE

The adjustment from civilian life to the rigid schedule of boot camp was not an easy one. Recruits trained six days a week for a total of 52 hours, plus the time they spent doing homework. Here is the daily routine, in the words of one recruit:

6 a.m.: Cannon shot to wake you

6:17: Lights glare on in barracks

6:30: After a masterful struggle you are dressed and at attention

7: March to mess

7:30: Make beds, wash latrines, dust, police grounds

8–12: Classes and close-order drill

12: More chow

1–4:30: Classes and physical education

5–5:30: Mess

9: Lights out in barracks

11: Bed check (and you had better be there)[7]

Women's Army Corps members unload supplies from a truck in North Africa.

Women's Army Corps (WAC). With this shift, women now received pay equal to that of their male counterparts. Women responded to the call of duty. In just one day, more than 13,000 women applied for 450 openings for officer candidates.[8] But this enthusiasm would not last. By the end of 1943, the numbers of women entering the service dwindled. The government fell far short of its 1943 goal of enlisting 150,000 women, with only 60,000 signing up.[9]

WOMEN PROVE THEMSELVES

Many assumed women would not be capable of doing military work, and the army was criticized for its decision to accept women. But WAC enlistees proved themselves more than capable.

Both Supreme Allied Commander General Douglas MacArthur and General Dwight D. Eisenhower were skeptical at first, but they later became impressed with the work ethic of the women. General MacArthur praised the women of WAC, calling them his "best soldiers."[10] Eisenhower, who was originally against women joining the military, changed his opinion by war's end. "Every phase of the record they compiled during the war convinced me of the error of my first reaction," he said.[11]

WAVES, SPARs, MARINES, AND WASPs

Other branches of the military soon accepted women as well. The navy established its own branch for women, nicknamed WAVES (Women Accepted for Volunteer Emergency Service), in July 1942. The coast guard launched SPAR (Semper Paratus—Always Ready) in November of the same year. The Marine Corps Women's Reserve (MCWR) began accepting female recruits in January 1943. In addition, female pilots served as members of Women Airforce Service Pilots (WASP).

The women who enlisted in WAVES received aviation training and worked as control tower operators, mechanics, parachute riggers, gunner's mates, and metalsmiths. WAVES also served in a wide variety of other areas including medicine, communications, and intelligence. The navy offered access to unique opportunities in the fields of science and mathematics that were not available through the other branches of the military. Grace Hopper, who went on to develop COBOL, a computer language, joined the Naval Reserve in December 1943 after teaching mathematics for more than a decade at Vassar College. With the navy, she worked to develop the first computers.

The first women to work for the coast guard were those who made sure the wicks stayed glowing in lighthouses along the coasts in the 1800s. During World War II, women enlisted as SPARs as official members of the coast guard. In addition to clerical work, some SPAR enlistees worked at Cape Cod on a top-secret navigation system called LORAN. SPARs had the distinction of being the only women in uniform during the war who were authorized to give orders to men—as long as the SPAR giving the order had a male commanding officer.

Female pilots with at least 500 hours of airtime were eligible to enlist in WASP. Although these women were not considered part of the military, they performed the important job of ferrying new planes from the factory to the aircraft carriers that would deliver them to bases overseas. They also served as flight instructors and test pilots, and they performed the dangerous task of towing targets for gunnery training.

NURSES CALLED TO DUTY

Without a doubt, the women who served in the most dangerous conditions during the war were nurses. And they were, more than any other women's branch of military service, the most visible and admired. Many members of the

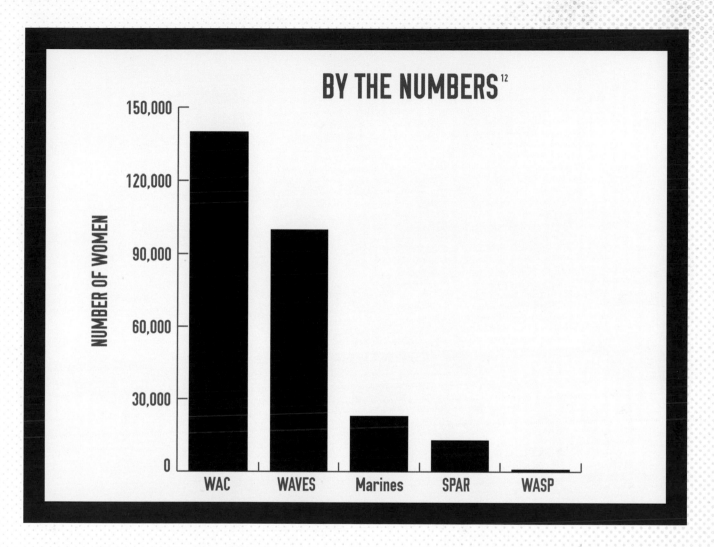

BY THE NUMBERS[12]

NUMBER OF WOMEN

| | WAC | WAVES | Marines | SPAR | WASP |

150,000
120,000
90,000
60,000
30,000
0

Army Nurse Corps (ANC), the Navy Nurse Corps (NNC), and flight nurses who were stationed abroad experienced firsthand life-and-death moments near the front lines. Those who served in Bataan, in the Philippines, tended to injured soldiers while rounds of artillery exploded around them. These nurses dug their own foxholes as protection against gunfire. They experienced hunger, fear, and

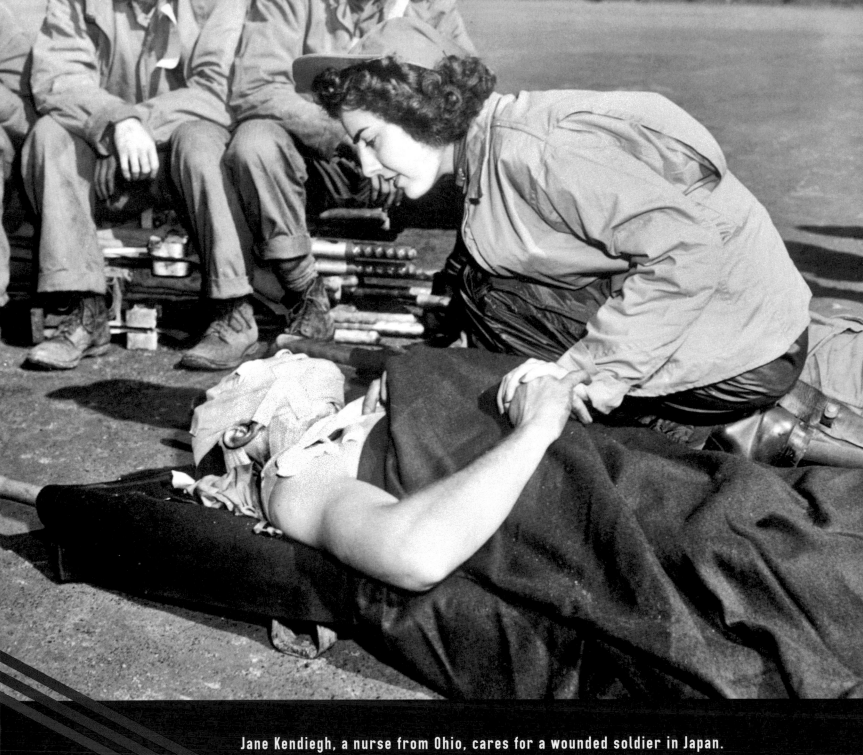

Jane Kendiegh, a nurse from Ohio, cares for a wounded soldier in Japan.

illnesses of their own. And when Corregidor, an island in the Philippines, was captured by the Japanese, army and navy nurses were captured and held as prisoners of war.

But nurses on the home front faced an uphill battle as well. It was a well-known fact that nurses worked long hours for very little pay. When wartime factory jobs became available, many nurses jumped at the opportunity to make more money in jobs with very little training required. A shortage of nurses throughout the United States in 1941 left 10,000 nursing jobs in hospitals vacant.[13] And with the war in Europe looming on the horizon, many more nurses would soon be needed for deployment overseas.

To draw women into the field of nursing, Ohio representative Frances Bolton proposed a bill that would pay for training nursing students. To take advantage of this opportunity, nurses had to commit to working through the duration of the war plus another six months. In June 1943, the bill was signed into law, creating a Cadet Nurse Corps program that funded nurse training and also provided students with uniforms.

But as the war dragged on, the desperate need for nurses continued. In fact, the need became so great President Roosevelt included in his 1945 State of the Union address an appeal for nurses to be drafted into service. However, the war ended before the bill passed.

The USO was founded in 1941 to boost morale for American soldiers. In addition to hosting dances, the USO also provided troops with movies, music, and comedy.

CHAPTER 6

LOVE AND MARRIAGE DURING WORLD WAR II

Heartbreak played out time and time again on train platforms across the United States as sweethearts and married couples said good-bye. As soldiers boarded the train for boot camp and likely deployment overseas, they had no idea if they would ever see their loved ones again—and if so, they did not know when. Under these circumstances, soldiers and their loved ones promised to write often. Husbands asked wives to send pictures and stories of their growing children. Then the women were left behind to work, wonder, and hope.

MARRIAGE RATES SPIKE

In these emotionally charged times, soldiers leaving for the front longed to establish a strong connection to someone at home.

Having a girlfriend or wife back home gave them something to live for. The rate of marriages in the United States increased sharply during the war years. Between 1939 and 1942, for example, marriage rates jumped 28 percent.[1] The rate continued to climb as the war raged on.

Dorothy Zmuda, an advertising layout artist, remembers young couples who barely knew each other rushing to get married. One young man, with whom she had gone on two dates to the movies, got word he was drafted and would be shipping out soon. When he arrived at her office with a ring, asking Zmuda for her hand in marriage, she was caught completely off guard. She told him no and explained that she did not know him well enough to marry him. The drafted soldier returned a couple of days later, brimming with the news that another girl had said yes. This kind of thing, Zmuda explained, happened all the time during the war years.

Men who did not want to go to war also had reason to get married. Married men, especially those with children, were more likely to be deferred from military service, at least during the war's early years. Women had to be especially careful in accepting hasty marriage proposals. There was always a chance the man was asking

FOLLOWING THE TROOPS

Some wives chose to follow their husbands wherever they were stationed in the United States. These women endured long cross-country train rides and often days of delay to stay with their loved ones. When she arrived in a military town, the soldier's wife faced a nearly impossible search for a decent place to live. Those with children had an even harder time finding a place. As military wives lived this leave-on-a-moment's-notice existence, they formed close bonds with other wives who were going through the same experiences.

A bride and groom stand outside the church after their wedding in 1943. The groom is wearing his military uniform.

for her hand simply to avoid being drafted. From 1939, when the draft began, until 1941, the government believed the increase in marriages was largely due to men who were attempting to avoid the draft.

But there were plenty of couples who got married during the war years simply because the time was right. They had planned to marry during the Great Depression but waited until the economy improved to exchange vows. In the

1930s and 1940s, a man was expected to be able to provide everything his new wife might need before asking her to marry.

ROMANCE IN WORDS

The women left behind did their best to keep their husbands or boyfriends updated on events at home through letters, telegrams, and an occasional phone call. Letters were also a way to maintain a romantic connection and declare affection for one another.

Flora Gaitree wrote often to her husband, Erman, who was stationed overseas with the army. Both Flora and Erman were journalists from Marietta, Georgia. In one letter to Erman, dated May 16, 1944, Flora explains the importance of their letters:

KEEPING A STIFF UPPER LIP

Throughout the war years, American women were instructed to smile and remain positive and upbeat in letters and calls to their loved ones overseas. Patriotic posters and advertisements produced by the Office of War Information appeared in every magazine, newspaper, and public space, reminding women that one of their primary tasks was to boost the morale of soldiers at home and abroad. One such poster read, "Keep Him Posted. Make it short. Make it cheerful. Send it V-mail."[2] One popular radio program ended each broadcast with the words, "Keep those letters flying to the boys overseas. Mail from home is the number one on their hit parade. They're doing the fighting. You do the writing."[3]

Erman dear:

Your grand letter arrived this morning and I had a glorious time lying in bed reading it. Our letters mean a lot to us, do they not darling? Somehow, by telling you everything just as it happens each day and reading your letters over and over again, I have a feeling of continuity so that when we are together again, even if it is only for a few hours we seem to resume our relationship . . . without any feeling of separation having preceded those hours. It is a glorious state and is one of the precious things about our marriage.[4]

REMAINING TRUE

Not all women married soldier boyfriends before they left for overseas deployment. Emily Koplin remembers many of her friends had boyfriends overseas. These young, single women considered themselves "tagged" and did not date other men while their boyfriends were away. They went to USO dances together as a group, though, and danced with the soldiers to do their part for the war effort.

There were some things, however, that couples did not share in letters. Many soldiers did not reveal any details about the horrors of battle, for fear they would worry loved ones back home. American pilot Quentin Aanenson nearly mailed a letter to his girlfriend, Jackie Greer, filled with these frightening details. With friends dying all around him and having just endured a fire in his plane in which he came very close to dying himself, Aanenson sat down and wrote to Greer:

I have purposely not told you much about my world over here, because I thought it might upset you. Perhaps that has been a mistake, so let me correct that right now. I still doubt if you will be able to comprehend it. I don't think anyone can who has not been through it. . . . I live in a world of death.[5]

But Aanenson could not bring himself to mail the letter. He felt it would be too hurtful for his girlfriend to read. Women on the home front sometimes chose not to share minor difficulties of their days, especially when it related to something their husbands usually took care of, such as a dripping faucet, an overdue bill, or the cold winter of 1944. These were small things that did not matter as much as getting the troops home safely, so they went unmentioned.

CENSORSHIP

During the war years, some topics were strictly forbidden, whether letter writers wanted to discuss them or not. Everyone knew letters to or from soldiers were not at all private. As is typically the case in times of war, the government censored all letters exchanged between the home front and troops overseas. Any letter writer could expect that someone in a government office would be opening the letter, reading it, and using a heavy black marker to cross out any details that could be considered harmful to the US military should the letter fall into enemy hands. These details included any mention of the location of troops, plans to ship out or fly out, attack plans, or even specifics about soldiers taking leave. The letter would then be resealed and sent off to its recipient.

Knowing the mail was censored, some couples devised their own code systems that enabled soldiers to let their loved ones know what they were doing. For example, a soldier might ask about the health of a specific uncle at home to let his wife know he would be going into battle soon.

Since soldiers were not allowed to reveal where they had been or where they were going, women on the home front followed the progress of American troops in the news. Like many women with a husband or loved one overseas, Vera Haney

Censors, many of whom were experienced linguists, read through letters, striking out any information that could help the enemy.

read Ernie Pyle's column, which featured regular updates by a down-to-earth American journalist on the front lines. She also listened to reports on the radio and read the newspaper. Sometimes she would go to the local movie theater just to watch the newsreels that played before the main feature. Using all of these sources and letters from her husband, Haney tried to track her husband's progress on a wall map of Europe.

WE REGRET TO INFORM YOU . . .

When the phone rang or someone knocked on the front door, women's worst fears would often surface. For Vera Haney, the telegram arrived nearly two weeks after her husband was killed in action in Germany. It read: "The secretary of war desires me to express his deep regret that your husband, Pfc, Haney, Joseph C., was killed in action in Germany 27 March 1945."[6]

Now a 26-year-old widow, Vera Haney had a four-year-old son to raise. Several of the letters she had sent over the past month were returned, marked "Deceased. Return to Sender." Months later, her husband's personal items arrived: a pair of glasses, a compass, a German army belt buckle, and photographs of Vera and her son with bloody fingerprints on the corners.

ERNIE PYLE

Ernie Pyle, a journalist and soldier from Dana, Indiana, wrote a daily newspaper column about his experiences alongside men fighting in World War II. In these columns, Pyle captured the daily life of soldiers—and for that reason, Americans back home became devoted readers. In his columns, Pyle told the truth. He said what soldiers could not bear to write in their own letters home. On April 18, 1945, Ernie Pyle was killed by enemy fire on Iejima, west of Okinawa. Americans mourned his death as if they had lost a good friend.

For the thousands and thousands of women on the home front who lost husbands or boyfriends during the war, life went on. Many World War II widows remarried, including Vera Haney. The wives and girlfriends of the more than

A young boy reads a letter from his father, who died in the sinking of an aircraft carrier in September 1942.

125,000 American soldiers who were taken as prisoners of war and the 73,000 who were declared missing in action had a harder time letting go and moving on with their lives.[7] Not knowing if they would ever see their loved ones again, these women remained stuck in limbo, grieving but still hanging on to a glimmer of hope that their loved ones would be found.

A mother holds her child while receiving nutrition advice from a visiting nurse.

MOTHERHOOD DURING WARTIME

"When is daddy coming home?" These words became all too familiar to wartime mothers. With husbands away at war, the women left behind had to raise their children and run the household alone. Those who went to work were expected to do it all, getting kids off to school or day care in time to punch in for a full day's work. Mothers with sons old enough to be drafted into military service endured a different kind of hardship. They waited and worried.

SENDING SONS OFF TO WAR

With so much focus on the war's effect on young brides and sweethearts, the media paid far less attention to the mothers who watched their sons march off to war. These women had watched their sons grow from babies to toddlers to schoolboys and finally into young men. All the hopes and dreams each mother had for her son were put on hold in the name of patriotism and serving country.

Mothers sometimes joined social groups for support. Organizations such as Blue Star Mothers of America, Mothers of Men in Service (MOMS), or Navy Mothers of World War II provided wartime mothers with a network of friends who could share experiences, worries, and concerns. In some parts of the country, these groups held social hours for moms and enlisted soldiers. It gave the men a chance to sit down and play a game of cards, have dinner, or simply talk with an American mom who had a son in the service. Five hundred men each week came for dinner with the Navy Mothers Club of Chicago.[1]

MOTHERHOOD NETWORKS

In the early 1940s, manufacturing shifted to producing munitions, aircraft, and ships instead of ordinary household goods—and that meant cribs, high chairs, diapers, and other baby items were in short supply. To fill this void, motherhood networks developed, especially among pregnant women. Mothers with toddlers passed down toys and clothing that their children had outgrown to friends or family members with younger babies.

Mothers supported each other, confided in each other, and shared ideas. Through these networks, young mothers formed meaningful friendships that lasted well beyond the war years. Jean Lechnir bonded with a group of young mothers during the war. They met once a week to play cards, and the tradition continued for another 48 years. In the 1940s, those who won a game got a pound of butter or a bag of sugar.

In some cases, mothers' hopes and dreams were dashed when sons never returned. The Sullivan family of Waterloo, Iowa, suffered unspeakable heartbreak when they learned all five sons—George, Francis, Joseph, Madison, and Albert—had died when the USS *Juneau* sank off the coast of the Solomon Islands in November 1942. The soldiers' mother, father, and two sisters did not officially learn of their deaths until seven months later. Then, a week before the death notices arrived, a neighbor shared a letter from her son who was also in the navy overseas. "Isn't it too bad about the Sullivan boys?" the son had written. "I heard that their ship was sunk."[2]

When the news finally came, Alleta Sullivan wrote down these thoughts:

> *In my first blind grief, it seemed as if almost everything I had lived for was gone. I couldn't eat or sleep. . . . I did find comfort in one thing they told me. I learned that everything had happened so fast that the boys must have died quickly and easily, without anguish or pain.*[3]

In other instances, mothers nursed their sons back to health or cared for sons who suffered permanent disabilities. Fortunately, many mothers had better

THE SULLIVAN FAMILY

After suffering such a great loss, the Sullivan family became quite famous. President Roosevelt wrote a personal letter to Mrs. Sullivan, expressing his condolences on the death of her sons. The navy asked the family if they would be willing to talk to workers at munitions and ordnance factories around the country as a way to rally employees to produce more for the war effort. The Sullivan brothers even appeared on posters stating, "The five Sullivan brothers 'missing in action' off the Solomons. *They* did their part."[4] The navy named two destroyer ships after the brothers, each of which was called USS *The Sullivans*. And in 1944, the movie *The Sullivans* told their story.

news. Their sons returned home and went on to lead happy, healthy lives.

CREATIVE SINGLE PARENTING

Mothers with young children faced an entirely different set of challenges. With their husbands away, these women became single parents. They had to balance their own traditional household tasks of caring for the children, cleaning the house, grocery shopping, and doing the laundry with those jobs that usually fell to the man of the house—handling the family finances, mowing the lawn, and fixing leaky faucets.

All of these ordinary chores were made more difficult by war shortages and rationing. Refrigerators, vacuum cleaners, toasters, washing machines, and other household appliances were not produced during the war years, so if one of these items failed, it could not be replaced

Alleta Sullivan reads a letter informing her that all five of her sons have been killed.

easily. Some mothers therefore resorted to the old way of doing things. When the refrigerator stopped running, they used an icebox. If the vacuum cleaner or washing machine stopped working, they used a broom or washed clothes by hand. These minor setbacks added more work to their already busy days.

Wartime shortages brought out a sense of creativity in many mothers. When socks wore through at the heels, mothers took out a needle and thread to mend them. While adults could make do with the clothes they had on hand, growing children could not. Although sewing machines were not available for purchase during the war, those who had them certainly used them. One mother used old kitchen curtains to make play clothes for her kids. Another used pieces from an old leather purse to patch worn-out elbows and knees on kids' clothing, extending the life of those pants and sweaters.

A WORKING MOTHER'S SCHEDULE

Even if their husbands were not fighting overseas, the demands of wartime meant many women had busy schedules. A woman named Alma worked the night shift so she could see her children off to school in the morning and meet them at the bus stop in the afternoon. Here is her schedule, which was common for mothers working during the war:

7 a.m.: Leave work and go to grocery store to get rationed meat before it sold out

8 a.m.: Kids fed, clothed, and off to school

9–10 a.m.: Eat breakfast, clean kitchen

10–11:30 a.m.: Nap

12 p.m.: Kids home from school, serve lunch

1–3 p.m.: Nap

3 p.m.: Kids home from school

3–6 p.m.: Clean house, do laundry, make dinner

6 p.m.: Husband home, dinner on the table

7–9:30 p.m.: Nap

10 p.m.: Leave for work[5]

DAY-CARE NEEDS

The vast majority of women with young children did not work outside the home during the war, but some mothers had to find jobs because money was tight. Those who did find work faced another obstacle: child care.

Although there were some factories that provided quality on-site day care for working mothers 24 hours a day, such as the Kaiser Company shipyards in Portland, Oregon, this practice was rare in the early 1940s. Many women were able to rely on their mothers, sisters, or friends to help with child care while they went to work. But for some, that was not an option. Some mothers worked the night shift, bringing their kids to work and leaving them in the car to sleep.

LIVING WITHOUT DAD

Perhaps a mother's toughest wartime duty was to keep memories of dad alive for her children. Mothers found themselves constantly fielding questions about when daddy would be coming home, whether he was safe, and where he was.

Isabel Alden wrote a letter to her husband, Maurice A. Kidder, sharing a story about their son Joel, who was seven at the time:

> *Joel was talking to me before he went to sleep last night and he said, "Do you know I'd like it better if Daddy went to work in the morning and came home every night." And I said I would too, only that thousands of little boys' "Daddies had to be gone at the war," and he said, "And thousands of them will get killed too." That old bugbear never leaves him. I always wish I could reassure him somehow, and whatever I do say seems so inadequate, like, "Well, all we can do is hope for the best."[6]*

Eleanor Green, a volunteer nurse, looks after a group of children while their mothers are at work.

DEALING WITH DEATH

Richard Haney was four years old when he grabbed the local paper off the front step and ran inside to show his mother, Vera. He was so excited to see his father's face on the front page. But what he did not know was that the article said his father had died in battle. When his mother saw the paper in his hands, she paused for a moment, smiled, and thanked him for bringing it in. She would tell him the terrible news later, of course, but now was not the time. Thousands of women found themselves in Vera's situation. Mothers constantly had to buffer their children against heartache and the cruelties of war, but they also had to find a way to gracefully tell them the truth.

For children who were too young to remember their fathers, mothers told stories about dad and described what he was like. Sometimes they made plans for fun activities they could do when dad returned, giving the children hope that they would see their father again.

In turn, wives did their best to keep their husbands updated on the lives of their children. Mothers took many photos of their children and encouraged kids to write notes or draw pictures to send along in letters to dad. But as the war dragged on, it was impossible not to lose some sense of the close-knit family they may have been before the war. Only when the family was reunited could they begin mending those gaps.

Mothers and their children read in the basement of an apartment building during a blackout drill.

A soldier kisses a young woman during V-J Day celebrations in New York City.

CHAPTER ★8★

AFTER THE WAR

On August 14, 1945, streets across the United States came alive with people dancing and celebrating. This date would go down in history as V-J Day—Victory in Japan Day—the day World War II finally came to an end. As they did with Pearl Harbor, Americans vividly remembered where they were when they heard the news. Ann McGhee Wilcox was with a girlfriend in San Francisco:

> *All of a sudden we looked up Market Street and all traffic had stopped. There was a wave of white coming down the street. We suddenly realized it was all sailors. A few soldiers were sprinkled in. I was swept off my feet, carried on shoulders for blocks. They wouldn't let me down. I had to find my girlfriend later. It was exciting, but it was scary.*[1]

The announcement that the war was over also rang out from loudspeakers in factories across the nation. At that moment, machines powered down and workers headed home. All wartime factories were closed until they could retool for civilian work.

The war had finally ended, and over the next few weeks, soldiers, including women who had served, began arriving home. Many of those who had left home to take jobs in faraway cities also returned. American families were thrilled to welcome back their loved ones. But the postwar years were a time of great transition for everyone on the home front. For women who had stayed behind, the adjustment to a peacetime economy in some ways meant taking a few steps backward. During the war, women had been encouraged to be independent and step up to work, volunteer, and do whatever was needed for the war. They had met these new challenges and been recognized for their efforts.

When the war ended, however, the government and the media began sending a different message—one that pushed for women to leave the workforce and return home. Men coming back from the war needed jobs. Veterans also expected life to be as it had been before they left. They wanted their wives to be at home,

THE OFFICE OF WAR INFORMATION

The Office of War Information (OWI) was a government agency created in June 1942. Through a monthly publication for the media called the *Magazine War Guide,* the OWI offered story ideas to magazine and newspaper editors. The OWI's main goal was to build "war-mindedness" and "solidarity" among Americans.[2] Many of the patriotic posters produced during the war years were the work of the OWI. But with the end of the war, the OWI shifted its focus. Posters calling for women to work the assembly line in the name of patriotism were replaced with those proclaiming that a woman's place is in the home.

not working all day on an assembly line or in an office. And returning soldiers wanted to buy a house, settle down, and start a family.

GIVING UP THE JOB

Women knew when they applied for wartime jobs that they would likely have to give them up when servicemen returned from the war. Vi Kirstine Vrooman, who worked as a riveter at Boeing Company in Seattle, Washington, remembers what it was like when the war ended:

> *After the war, most of the workers went back to Oklahoma. And when the guys came back, the women all went home and did the dishes. There was no question about that. None of the women said, "I don't want to lose this job. I want to stay here and do this. I want to get this big money." They didn't. It was like an unwritten law. They just packed their little tool kits and went back home.*[3]

There were many women who accepted the new reality and looked forward to staying home and raising children. But there were others who liked the feeling of independence they got from working away from home. They did not necessarily want to stay at the same jobs they had during the war, but they did like the idea of having a job and getting out of the house. In fact, 75 percent of the working women surveyed during the war stated that they would rather keep working than return to life as a full-time homemaker.[4]

After the soldiers returned home, these women were expected to leave their factory jobs.

A WOMAN'S PLACE IS IN THE HOME

With the men back to fill jobs on the home front, businessmen, government officials, and labor leaders advised women to stop working. Social workers suggested that women needed to pay closer attention to their children. Working women were blamed for rising instances of juvenile delinquency, divorce, and children born to unmarried mothers. Just as a woman's job during the war was to work and volunteer, her role in postwar times was to stay home to run the household and maintain a sense of order within the family.

Most women fell back into the role of homemaker with relative ease. Modern time-saving appliances such as washing machines, electric sweepers, and gas stoves took some of the extra work out of household tasks. But the job was by no means easy. Women's magazines, advertisements, and newspaper articles offered endless advice to American women about the best diet for growing children, how to raise kids properly, what household products one should not be without, and the best ways to decorate the home. And women who worked outside the home were not excused from housework. While

THE UNDERSTANDING WIFE

One of the roles the wives of returning soldiers were expected to fulfill was that of understanding wife and sometimes therapist to husbands who had suffered the psychological stress of war. The government urged women to do whatever they could to support their husbands and ease their transition to civilian life—even if that meant quitting a job they loved in order to be at home. Sociologists and psychiatrists at the time recommended that women set aside their own needs for the sake of their husbands' happiness.

full-time homemakers typically spent 56 hours per week on housework, working women usually spent 34 hours per week cleaning, cooking, or doing laundry.[5]

SETTLING DOWN

Many American soldiers returned from war ready to settle down and raise a family. Millions of veterans took advantage of the G.I. Bill, a piece of legislation enacted in June 1944 that gave returning military personnel access to low-interest loans for homes, businesses, or farms and provided funding for education. Veterans purchased new homes, often in suburbs such as Levittown, Pennsylvania. Such neighborhoods were made up of tract houses—basic, mass-produced homes that were built quickly and cheaply. Although the homes were small, the loans offered through the G.I. Bill often made them a cheaper option than renting an apartment in the city. Owning a home had been an impossible dream for most Americans before the war, but with the help of the G.I. Bill, almost 2.4 million veterans received home loans between 1944 and 1952.[6]

But having a new house and a yard with a modern kitchen was not always what women dreamed it would be. These

G.I. BILL

Signed into law by President Roosevelt in June 1944, the G.I. Bill did more than provide returning soldiers with low-interest loans for homes, businesses, or farms. It also provided funding for education and training, job-search help, and weekly unemployment payments while veterans looked for work. Amendments to the bill also allotted money for building Veterans Administration hospitals around the country. These benefits went a long way toward helping soldiers settle back into civilian life at home. Although the bill did apply to female veterans, women made up only about 2 percent of the armed forces.[7] This meant the benefits awarded to veterans overwhelmingly applied to men instead of women.

Newly constructed suburbs often featured rows and rows of similar-looking houses.

suburban homes were often located far from city centers, making it difficult for women to socialize and participate in community activities. For some women, this was a recipe for loneliness.

Nine months after soldiers returned home, the first wave of postwar babies arrived. In 1946, a record-breaking 3.4 million babies were born to American women, a 20 percent increase over the year before.[8] These babies were the first of what is called the baby boom generation, which lasted until 1964. In the final decade of the baby boom, 4 million babies were born each year.[9] For the first time in years, American couples felt confident about bringing children into the world. The economy was still booming, holding the promise of jobs for years to come. Modern conveniences made housekeeping a little easier for young mothers. And it looked, at least for a while, as if the new peace would continue.

ROCKY REUNIONS

After months and often years apart, many couples had to get to know each other all over again. The experiences each person had during the war shaped and sometimes changed who they were. Women on the home front were expected to be supportive and understanding of the hardships their husbands had endured during the war. But often little thought was given to the sacrifices women made at home and how their experiences may have changed them.

Edith Sokol was the director of a day-care center in Cleveland, Ohio. In a letter to her husband, Victor Speert, she tried to explain how the war had changed her:

> Last night Mel and I were talking about some of the adjustments we'll have to make to our husbands' return. I must admit I'm not exactly the same girl you left—I'm twice as independent as I used to be and to top it off, I sometimes think I've become "hard as nails." . . . Also—more and more I've been living exactly as I want to, and I don't see people I don't care about—I do as I damn please. As a whole, I don't think my changes will affect our relationship, but I do think you'll have to remember that there are some slight alterations in me. I'm pretty sure that holds true for you too—am I correct?[10]

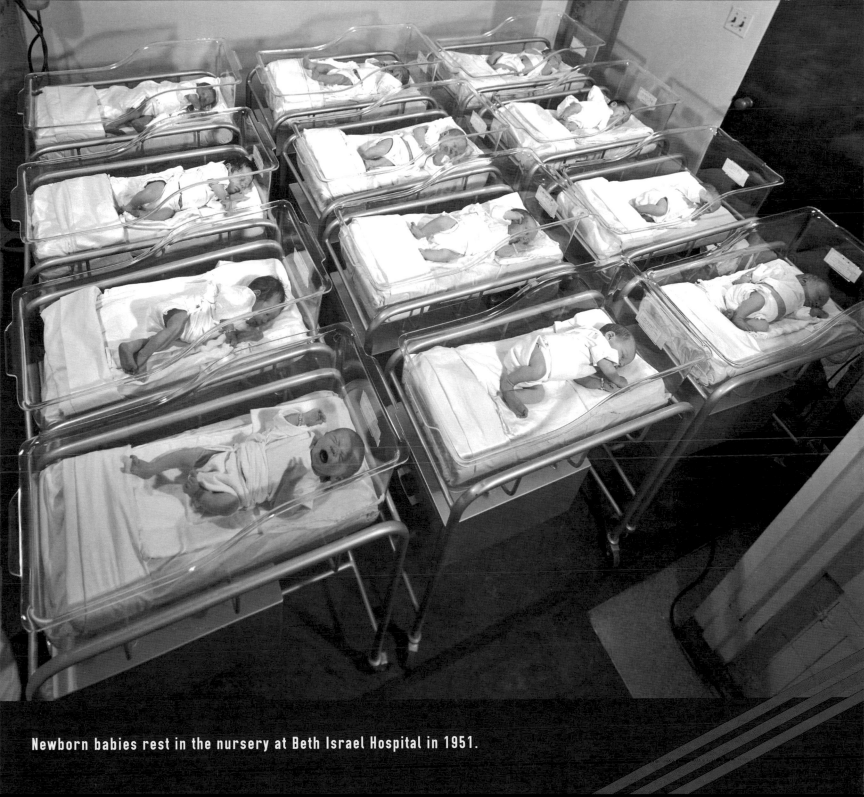

Newborn babies rest in the nursery at Beth Israel Hospital in 1951.

While many couples were able to bridge these differences and move on to create a new life together, others were not so lucky. Divorce rates soared in the years immediately following the war. Of the 2.3 million weddings that took place in 1946, 600,000 of them ended in divorce.[11]

THE ROLE OF WOMEN

From 1941 until 1945, women were called on to fill in for men in roles never thought possible before the war. They became welders, factory workers, crane operators, managers, scientists, college professors, mechanics, pilots, volunteers, gardeners, and community organizers. They worked hard, and they did their jobs well. Women carried this new sense of self-confidence within them long after the war had ended.

The experiences that many women had during the war years demonstrated their ability to excel in a wide range of jobs. It also showed that they could run a household on their own if necessary and serve their country as equal citizens. This realization would leave a lasting impression, which proved invaluable to the

WOMEN IN THE MEDIA

Postwar movies and advertisements drove home the message that women should be at home. Many ads portrayed women at home, happily spending time with family and doing housework. In one advertisement for Singer sewing machines, back in production with the war's end, a husband hugs his wife as she lunges toward the sewing machine, looking as if she cannot wait to sit down and begin sewing clothes for the entire family. The caption reads, "Rub your eyes, honey—it's a brand-new Singer!"[12]

More than two decades after World War II ended, marchers took to the streets demanding equality for women.

new women's movement that emerged in the 1960s. These changes would not have been possible without the lessons and growth women experienced during the years of World War II.

TIMELINE

September 1940

Congress institutes the Selective Training and Service Act, officially drafting soldiers into the US armed services.

June 1941

Roosevelt signs Executive Order 8802, prohibiting defense industry discrimination on the basis of race.

November 24, 1941

A young woman knitting is featured on the cover of *Life* magazine, calling for Americans to knit 1 million sweaters by Christmas.

December 1941

After Japan attacks Pearl Harbor, Hawaii, American factories begin to retool for the war effort.

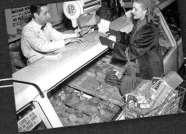

November 1942

SPAR is established.

January 1943

Marines accept women into service.

March 1943

Processed foods, meats, cheese, and butter are rationed.

May 29, 1943

Norman Rockwell's Rosie the Riveter illustration appears on the front cover of the *Saturday Evening Post*.

January 1942

The United States rations rubber; women begin accepting jobs in the war industry.

February 1942

Civilian car production is halted.

May 1942

Congress institutes the Women's Army Auxiliary Corps (WAAC).

July 1942

WAVES is established; the first WAAC recruits report for boot camp in Des Moines, Iowa.

June 1943

President Roosevelt signs a bill providing funding for nurses through the Cadet Nurse Corps program.

June 1944

President Roosevelt signs the G.I. Bill into law.

August 14, 1945

World War II comes to an end with victory over Japan, prompting wartime factories to stop production.

1946

American women give birth to 3.4 million babies, signifying the start of the baby boom.

ESSENTIAL FACTS

KEY PLAYERS

- Rosie the Riveter is the iconic image of a female wartime munitions worker that appeared on patriotic posters designed to entice American women to go to work for the war effort.

- Eleanor Roosevelt serves as First Lady of the United States from 1933 through 1945, during which time she champions the rights of women, the poor, and the underprivileged.

- Oveta Culp Hobby, a journalist, lawyer, and women's rights advocate, becomes director of the Women's Army Auxiliary Corps in 1942.

KEY STATISTICS

- More than 400,000 women leave housework behind to begin manufacturing weapons, ammunition, ships, planes, and other supplies needed on the front lines.

- From 1940 through 1945, the number of American women in the labor force increases by more than 50 percent, peaking at 19 million in July 1944.

- An estimated 30 million Americans move away from home in the 1940s, many to take new jobs or join the military.

- In 1946, 2.3 million weddings take place in the United States.

IMPACT ON THE WAR

Due to the efforts of American women, the United States is able to fulfill wartime manufacturing needs and keep its businesses and government running. Women step in to fill noncombat positions in the military, such as gunnery instruction, parachute packing, and radio operations, allowing men to focus their efforts on fighting. By tending Victory gardens and getting creative with cooking, women make up for the food shortfalls that occur due to rationing.

IMPACT ON SOCIETY

The successes women experience while meeting the challenges of World War II provide them with the confidence and know-how to fight for women's equality in the 1960s and beyond.

QUOTE

"You gain strength, courage, and confidence by every experience in which you really stop to look fear in the face. . . . *You must do the thing you think you cannot do.*"

—*Eleanor Roosevelt*

GLOSSARY

CENSOR

To prevent specific information from reaching certain people.

CRYPTOGRAPHER

A person who makes codes or tries to break other people's codes.

DRAFT

A system in which people of a certain age are required to register for military service.

HOMEMAKER

Someone who stays home and cleans, does laundry, cooks, and raises children rather than work outside the home. In the 1940s, homemakers were almost always women.

INDUCTION

The process of placing someone into the armed services.

MUNITIONS

Bombs, bullets, shells, and other objects that are shot from weapons.

ORDNANCE FACTORY

A factory that manufactures artillery shells and explosives for use in war.

PATRIOTISM

A strong sense of responsibility and devotion to one's country.

RATIONING

Setting limits on the amount of certain foods or materials a population can purchase during war or other conflicts.

STIPEND

A fixed, regular payment for a service performed.

VICTORY GARDEN

A type of garden planted during World War II to help make up for the shortage of fresh fruits and vegetables brought on by the war effort and rationing.

WAR BOND

A bond sold by the government while a nation is at war to finance military activities.

ADDITIONAL RESOURCES

SELECTED BIBLIOGRAPHY

Haney, Richard Carlton. *"When Is Daddy Coming Home?" An American Family during World War II*. Madison, WI: Wisconsin Historical Society, 2005. Print.

Litoff, Judy Barrett, and David C. Smith, eds. *Since You Went Away: World War II Letters from American Women on the Home Front*. New York: Oxford UP, 1991. Print.

Wise, Nancy Baker, and Christy Wise. *A Mouthful of Rivets: Women at Work in World War II*. San Francisco: Jossey-Bass, 1994. Print.

FURTHER READINGS

Atwood, Kathryn J. *Women Heroes of World War II: 26 Stories of Espionage, Sabotage, Resistance, and Rescue*. Chicago: Chicago Review, 2011. Print.

Fleming, Candace. *Our Eleanor: A Scrapbook Look at Eleanor Roosevelt's Remarkable Life*. New York: Atheneum, 2005. Print.

Mullenbach, Cheryl. *Double Victory: How African American Women Broke Race and Gender Barriers to Help Win World War II*. Chicago: Chicago Review, 2013. Print.

WEBSITES

To learn more about Essential Library of World War II, visit **booklinks.abdopublishing.com**. These links are routinely monitored and updated to provide the most current information available.

Fort Hancock, Gateway National Recreation Area
26 Hudson Avenue
Highlands, NJ 07732
732-872-5970
http://www.nps.gov/gate/historyculture/wwiiforthancock.htm
Visit this historic fort that was home to 70 WAC members, the first of whom arrived on June 23, 1943. The female recruits worked at the Fort Hancock post exchange, motor pool, post headquarters, mess hall, commissary, finance office, and dental office.

Rosie the Riveter WWII Home Front National Historical Park
1414 Harbour Way South #3000
Richmond, CA 94804
510-232-5050
http://www.nps.gov/rori/index.htm
Based in Richmond, California, and home to four active shipyards during World War II, this park provides visitors a glimpse into what it may have been like to work as a shipbuilder in the 1940s.

SOURCE NOTES

CHAPTER 1. A NATION AT WAR

1. "The World Today: Pearl Harbor Attack, December 7, 1941, 2:31 pm EST." *AuthenticHistory.com*. AuthenticHistory.com, n.d. Web. 27 Feb. 2015.

2. Elizabeth P. McIntosh. "Honolulu after Pearl Harbor: A Report Published for the First Time, 71 Years Later." *Washington Post*. Washington Post, 6 Dec. 2012. Web. 27 Feb. 2015.

3. Patricia Dooley. "Life on the Home Front through the Eyes of Myrtle Fortun." *Roots* 17.2 (1989): 8. Print.

4. Michael E. Stevens. *Voices of the Wisconsin Past: Women Remember the War 1941–1945*. Madison, WI: Wisconsin Historical Society, 1993. Print. 6.

5. "Pearl Harbor." *History.com*. A&E Television Networks, n.d. Web. 27 Feb. 2015.

6. "December 8, 1941: The United States declares war on Japan." *History.com*. A&E Television Networks, n.d. Web. 27 Feb. 2015.

7. "By the Numbers: The US Military." *The National WWII Museum*. The National WWII Museum, n.d. Web. 27 Feb. 2015.

8. "September 16, 1940: United States Imposes the Draft." *History.com*. A&E Television Networks, n.d. Web. 27 Feb. 2015.

9. "By the Numbers: The US Military." *The National WWII Museum*. The National WWII Museum, n.d. Web. 27 Feb. 2015.

10. Joyce Bryant. "How War Changed the Role of Women in the United States." *Yale-New Haven Teacher's Institute*. Yale-New Haven Teacher's Institute, 3 Feb. 2009. Web. 27 Feb. 2015.

11. Richard Carlton Haney. *"When Is Daddy Coming Home?" An American Family during World War II*. Madison, WI: Wisconsin Historical Society, 2005. Print. 61.

CHAPTER 2. A NOT-SO-EVERYDAY LIFE

1. "World War II Rationing on the U.S. Homefront." *Ames Historical Society*. Ames Historical Society, n.d. Web. 27 Feb. 2015.

2. Ibid.

3. Richard Carlton Haney. *"When Is Daddy Coming Home?" An American Family during World War II*. Madison, WI: Wisconsin Historical Society, 2005. Print. 6.

4. Michael E. Stevens. *Voices of the Wisconsin Past: Women Remember the War 1941–1945*. Madison, WI: Wisconsin Historical Society, 1993. Print. 82.

5. "Wartime Cookery." *Ames Historical Society*. Ames Historical Society, n.d. Web. 27 Feb. 2015.

6. "The Home Front." *Wessels Living History Farm*. Wessels Living History Farm, n.d. Web. 27 Feb. 2015.

7. "Blackouts Darken the Skies of Oregon." *Life on the Home Front: Oregon Responds to World War II*. Oregon Secretary of State, n.d. Web. 27 Feb. 2015.

8. Tim O'Neil. "A Look Back: World War II Blackout Drill Darkens St. Louis." *St. Louis Post-Dispatch*. St. Louis Post-Dispatch, 16 Dec. 2012. Web. 27 Feb. 2015.

9. "Clinton in World War II." *Clinton Historical Society*. Clinton Historical Society, 8 Mar. 2004. Web. 27 Feb. 2015.

10. "World War II Rationing on the U.S. Homefront." *Ames Historical Society*. Ames Historical Society, n.d. Web. 27 Feb. 2015.

CHAPTER 3. WOMEN GO TO WORK

1. Susan Hartmann. *The Home Front and Beyond: American Women in the 1940s*. Boston: Twayne, 1982. Print. 21.

2. Thomas C. Thompson "War, Women, and Lipstick." *Roots* 17.2 (1989): 27–35. Print.

3. "World War II Posters: Women." *About.com: 20th Century History*. About.com, n.d. Web. 27 Feb. 2015.

4. Susan Hartmann. *The Home Front and Beyond: American Women in the 1940s*. Boston: Twayne, 1982. Print. 79.

5. "Arsenal of Democracy." *Encyclopedia of Detroit*. Detroit Historical Society, n.d. Web. 27 Feb. 2015.

6. "Rosie the Riveter." *History.com*. A&E Television Networks, n.d. Web. 27 Feb. 2015.

7. "Executive Order 8802." *The First Measured Century*. PBS, n.d. Web. 27 Feb. 2015.

8. Gordon J. Hylton. "Adam's Rib as an Historical Document: The Plight of Women Lawyers in the 1940s." *Marquette University Law School Faculty Blog*. Marquette University Law School Faculty Blog, n.d. Web. 27 Feb. 2015.

9. "War, Women, and Opportunity." *Women Come to the Front*. Library of Congress, n.d. Web. 27 Feb. 2015.

10. "Japanese American Incarceration Facts." *Japanese American National Museum*. Japanese American National Museum, n.d. Web. 27 Feb. 2015.

11. Michael E. Stevens. *Women Remember the War, 1941–1945*. Madison, WI: Wisconsin Historical Society, 1993. Print. 10–11.

12. Judy Barrett Litoff and David C. Smith, eds. *American Women in a World at War: Contemporary Accounts from World War II*. Wilmington, DE: Scholarly Resources, 1997. Print. 194.

CHAPTER 4. VOLUNTEERING FOR THE WAR EFFORT

1. "American Gardener: Victory Gardens." *Terrain*. Terrain, 12 July 2013. Web. 27 Feb. 2015.

2. David Walbert. "Victory Gardens." *Learn NC*. Learn NC, n.d. Web. 27 Feb. 2015.

3. "Victory Gardens." *Wessels Living History Farm*. Wessels Living History Farm, n.d. Web. 27 Feb. 2015.

4. "Gardens for US at War: Six Million Amateurs Work the Soil." *Life*. 30 March 1942: 81–84. Print.

5. "Victory Gardens." *Wessels Living History Farm*. Wessels Living History Farm, n.d. Web. 27 Feb. 2015.

6. "The Scotts on the Home Front." *Within These Walls . . . 1 House, 5 Families, 200 Years of History*. Smithsonian National Museum of American History, n.d. Web. 27 Feb. 2015.

7. "Gardens for US at War: Six Million Amateurs Work the Soil." *Life*. 30 March 1942: 82–83. Print.

8. Eleanor Roosevelt. *You Learn By Living*. Philadelphia: Westminster, 1960. Print. 29–30.

9. "Knitting for Victory: World War II." *Essay 5722*. HistoryLink.org, n.d. Web. 27 Feb. 2015.

10. "Communication: Letters & Diaries." *The War*. PBS, n.d. Web. 27 Feb. 2015.

11. "'My Dearest Husband': How V-mail Changed War Communication." *The National WWII Museum*. The National WWII Museum, n.d. Web. 27 Feb. 2015.

12. "War Bonds for the War Effort." *The National WWII Museum*. The National WWII Museum, n.d. Web. 27 Feb. 2015.

13. "Reflections: Wartime Bond Drives." *Army Historical Foundation*. Army Historical Foundation, n.d. Web. 27 Feb. 2015.

CHAPTER 5. WOMEN IN THE SERVICE

1. "Women in World War II at a Glance: On the Home Front and Beyond." *The National WWII Museum*. The National WWII Museum, n.d. Web. 27 Feb. 2015.

2. "The Women's Army Corps." *Sandy Hook*. National Park Service, US Department of the Interior, n.d. Web. 27 Feb. 2015.

3. "Oveta Culp Hobby." *Encyclopaedia Britannica*. Encyclopaedia Britannica, 3 March 2014. Web. 27 February 2015.

4. "Focus On: Women at War." *The National WWII Museum*. The National WWII Museum, n.d. Web. 27 Feb. 2015.

5. "World War II: Women's Army Corps." *Women in Military Service for America Memorial*. Women in Military Service for America Memorial, n.d. Web. 27 Feb. 2015.

6. Colonel Betty Morden. "Women's Army Corps." *Women in Military Service for America Memorial*. Women in Military Service for America Memorial, n.d. Web. 27 Feb. 2015.

7. Doris Weatherford. *American Women and World War II*. New York: Facts on File, 1990. Print. 51.

8. "The Women's Army Corps." *Sandy Hook*. National Park Service, U.S. Department of the Interior, n.d. Web. 27 Feb. 2015.

9. Doris Weatherford. *American Women and World War II*. New York: Facts on File, 1990. Print. 34.

10. "World War II: Women and the War." *Women in Military Service for America Memorial*. Women in Military Service for America Memorial, n.d. Web. 27 Feb. 2015.

11. Ibid.

12. Susan Hartmann. *The Home Front and Beyond: American Women in the 1940s*. Boston: Twayne, 1982. Print. 32.

13. Doris Weatherford. *American Women and World War II*. New York: Facts on File, 1990. Print. 16.

CHAPTER 6. LOVE AND MARRIAGE DURING WORLD WAR II

1. Michael E. Stevens. *Women Remember the War, 1941–1945*. Madison, WI: Wisconsin Historical Society, 1993. Print. 6.

2. Judy Barrett Litoff and David C. Smith, eds. *Since You Went Away: World War II Letters from American Women on the Home Front*. Wichita, KS: U of Kansas P, 1995. Print. 123.

3. Ibid. 126.

4. Ibid. 114–115.

5. "Communication: Letters & Diaries." *The War*. PBS, n.d. Web. 27 Feb. 2015.

6. Richard Carlton Haney. "When Is Daddy Coming Home?" *An American Family during World War II*. Madison, WI: Wisconsin Historical Society, 2005. Print. 87.

7. Doris Weatherford. *American Women and World War II.* New York: Facts on File, 1990. Print. 297.

CHAPTER 7. MOTHERHOOD DURING WARTIME

1. Doris Weatherford. *American Women and World War II.* New York: Facts on File, 1990. Print. 300.

2. Ibid. 298.

3. Ibid. 299.

4. "The Five Sullivan Brothers, 'Missing in Action' off the Solomons: They Did Their Part." *UNT Digital Library.* University of North Texas, n.d. Web. 27 Feb. 2015.

5. Doris Weatherford. *American Women and World War II.* New York: Facts on File, 1990. Print. 163.

6. Judy Barrett Litoff and David C. Smith, eds. *Since You Went Away: World War II Letters from American Women on the Home Front.* Wichita, KS: U of Kansas P, 1995. Print. 96.

CHAPTER 8. AFTER THE WAR

1. Nancy Baker Wise and Christy Wise. *A Mouthful of Rivets: Women at Work in World War II.* San Francisco: Jossey-Bass, 1994. Print. 200.

2. Maureen Honey. "New Roles for Women and the Feminine Mystique: Popular Fiction of the 1940s." *American Studies* 24.1 (1983): 41, 45. Print.

3. Nancy Baker Wise and Christy Wise. *A Mouthful of Rivets: Women at Work in World War II.* San Francisco: Jossey-Bass, 1994. Print. 195–196.

4. Thomas C. Thompson "War, Women, and Lipstick." *Roots* 17.2 (1989): 27–35. Print.

5. Susan Hartmann. *The Home Front and Beyond: American Women in the 1940s.* Boston: Twayne, 1982. Print. 168.

6. "About G.I. Bill: History and Timeline." *US Department of Veterans Affairs.* US Department of Veterans Affairs, n.d. Web. 27 Feb. 2015.

7. Susan Hartmann. *The Home Front and Beyond: American Women in the 1940s.* Boston: Twayne, 1982. Print. 26.

8. "Baby Boomers." *History.com.* A&E Television Networks, n.d. Web. 27 Feb. 2015.

9. Ibid.

10. Judy Barrett Litoff and David C. Smith, eds. *Since You Went Away: World War II Letters from American Women on the Home Front.* Wichita, KS: U of Kansas P, 1995. Print. 157.

11. Susan Hartmann. *The Home Front and Beyond: American Women in the 1940s.* Boston: Twayne, 1982. Print. 165.

12. Thomas C. Thompson "War, Women, and Lipstick." *Roots* 17.2 (1989): 27–35. Print.

INDEX

ABOUT THE AUTHOR

Kari Cornell is a freelance writer and editor who loves to read, garden, cook, run, and make clever things out of nothing. She is the author of *The Nitty Gritty Gardening Book: Fun Projects for All Seasons*, six *You're the Chef* cookbooks for kids, and *Growing with Purpose: Forty Years of Seward Community Cooperative*. She lives in Minneapolis, Minnesota, with her husband, Brian, two sons, Will and Theo, and her crazy dog, Emmylou.